If I Can See It, I Can Do It A Memoir

By
Roman Sewell

ISBN: 978 -1-0369-7447-3
Printed in the United Kingdom

Contents

Chapter One – Shadows of Childhood

Chapter Two – Lost and Not Found

Chapter Three – Behind Prison

Chapter Four – Recovery and Rebuilding

Chapter Five – Living My Truth

Chapter Six – Closing Reflections

About the Author

Dedication

To my mum, It took many years for us to find each other again
— To rebuild what life once tore apart.
But love found its way back, and I'll always carry her in my heart.
Your resilience became the backbone of my own,
and your belief in me planted the first seed of hope that maybe, one day,
I could become the person I was always meant to be

To my sister — my rock, my constant —
Your love has been the light that never
faded.
Thank you for being my anchor when the world felt overwhelming.
You saw me in ways no one else did — not the chaos, not the

mistakes, not the pain —
but the heart behind it all.
Your support wasn't loud, but it was steady, constant, and honest.
You reminded me that family isn't just blood; it's loyalty, understanding, and the courage to hold space for someone while they're figuring out who they are.
You gave me room to grow, room to break, and room to become whole again.

To Eco-Actif

You were the turning point.
At a time when I was still carrying my past like a weight around my neck, you looked at me and saw something else — potential, purpose, strength, and a future worth investing in.
You gave me space to be useful, to contribute, to rediscover parts of myself that had been buried under years of survival.
You didn't treat me like a case, a statistic, or a risk.
You treated me like a human being with something valuable to offer.

You didn't just support me —
you gave me the courage to support others.
You helped me realise that my past didn't make me unworthy;
it made me powerful.
It gave me the tools to understand people who were lost, hurting, or starting again.
It gave me the strength to stand beside them, not above them.

And because of the faith you placed in me, because of the confidence you helped rebuild, I found the courage to create something of my own —
Reformed East Sussex.

A place built on belief, compassion, and second chances.
A place that exists because you showed me what hope can look like when someone invests in it.

Acknowledgements

There are so many people who played a part in this journey — people who stood beside me, behind me, and even in front of me when I needed guiding more than I needed walking. To all of you, this book is as much yours as it is mine.

I would like to thank everyone who supported me through the moments when I didn't know who I was becoming, when my past felt too heavy to carry, and when my future felt uncertain. You loved me through confusion, celebrated my growth, and held space for my truth long before I learned to stand confidently in it myself.

To my friends — thank you for seeing me beyond the chaos of my past and choosing to stay, even when staying wasn't the easiest option. Your loyalty helped me rebuild trust in a world where trust had once been dangerous. Your conversations, your humour, your honesty, and your presence reminded me that connection is still possible even after a life spent surviving.

To my family and new found family — thank you for your patience, for your unconditional love, and for giving me the foundation I once thought I'd lost. You carried the weight of my silence, my struggles, and the many versions of me that came and went as I tried to find my way. Thank you for not giving up, even when I didn't understand myself enough to explain what was happening inside me.

To those who believed in me when I could not believe in myself — your faith became the quiet voice I needed in the darkest moments. The reassurance you offered, even in the simplest ways, helped me move forward when turning back felt easier.

To the people who crossed my path for only a moment, yet left a lasting impact — thank you. Sometimes it was a single conversation, a kind word, or a moment of understanding that shifted something in me. You may never know what you contributed, but I carry it with me.

To Eco-Actif — your role in my story goes far beyond employment or support. You helped me relearn how to show up in the world. You gave me purpose when I had lost mine, belief when mine was shattered, and structure when life felt uncertain. You saw a leader inside me long before I saw it myself. Your encouragement helped plant the first seeds of Reformed East Sussex, and for that, I will forever be grateful.

To Reformed East Sussex — not just the organisation, but every single person who walked through its doors. You trusted me with your stories, your fears, your hopes, and your second chances. You helped shape my understanding of strength, resilience, and what it means to rebuild. You reminded me that change is not only possible — it is powerful. You inspired me as much as I hope I have inspired you.

To the professionals, mentors, and quiet supporters who offered guidance along the way — thank you. Your insight and gentleness helped me navigate a world that once felt too loud for me.

And finally, to anyone who has ever felt lost, misunderstood, unseen, or unsure of who they are allowed to become — thank you for existing. Thank you for fighting to stay alive. Thank you for giving stories like mine a place to land. I hope this book reminds you that you are not alone, that growth is real, that transformation is possible, and that your story matters more than you know.

This journey has been shaped by countless hands and countless hearts.
I may have written these words, but I did not walk this path alone.
Thank you — all of you — for helping me find my voice, my truth, and my life.

FOREWORD

There are stories that entertain, stories that educate, and stories that leave a mark that stays with you long after the final page is turned. Roman's story is the third kind — a life lived in the shadows of trauma, survival, transformation, and ultimately truth. This is not just a memoir of hardship; it is a testament to human resilience and the courage it takes to rebuild not just a life, but a self.

Roman's honesty is disarming. He does not shy away from the darker parts of his journey, nor does he exaggerate them. Instead, he tells his truth with clarity, compassion, and a strength that comes from lived experience. What makes his story remarkable is not what he endured, but what he chose to become despite it.

His path has not been linear. It has been messy, raw, uncertain, but always moving forward. Through addiction, homelessness, incarceration, loss, identity struggles, and the weight of a world that demanded he be someone he never was, Roman emerged with a voice that lifts others. His work with Reformed East Sussex shows not only his strength, but his heart — a heart built for service, for empathy, for guiding those who walk the same difficult roads he once did.

This book is a reminder that transformation is possible, that identity can be rediscovered, and that hope is not a luxury — it's a lifeline. Roman does not preach; he speaks. He does not instruct; he shares. And through that sharing, he hands the reader something rare: permission to believe in their own ability to change.

You will not finish this book the same person you were when you began it.
Roman's story will stay with you.
And it should.

PREFACE

I never planned to write this book. For many years, my story felt too heavy, too complicated, too painful to put into words. I carried it quietly, believing that silence meant strength. I believed survival was enough.

But survival is not living.

As I rebuilt my life — piece by piece, truth by truth — I began to understand that telling my story wasn't about revisiting the past. It was about reclaiming it. It was about giving voice to the parts of me that were never allowed to speak, the identity I hid, the pain I buried, and the resilience I didn't know I had.

This book is not written from a place of perfection. It is written from a place of honesty. A place where shame no longer holds power. A place where growth is real, and transformation is possible. My hope is that my journey — messy, imperfect, and human — helps someone else see that theirs matters too.

AUTHOR'S NOTE

This memoir contains parts of my life that were extremely difficult to live, and sometimes even more difficult to revisit. I have tried to tell my story with truth and respect — for myself, for those who walked alongside me, and for those who could not.

Some names and identifying details have been altered to protect privacy.
The experiences, emotions, and lessons are real.

I am not writing as a victim or a hero.
I am writing as a human being who refused to stay broken.

If you see yourself in these pages — in the pain, the confusion, the identity struggles, the rebuilding — please know this: there is nothing wrong with you. You are not alone. You are allowed to grow. You are allowed to change. You are allowed to become who you truly are.

Thank you for reading my truth.

A LETTER TO THE READER

Dear Reader,

Thank you for picking up this book — whether by curiosity, instinct, or the hope of finding something within these pages that speaks to you.

I want you to know that this is not just my story.
It is a reminder that every person has the capacity to rebuild.
Every person has the right to discover who they truly are.
And every person deserves a life that feels like their own.

You might be reading this because you've lived through hard things.
Maybe you're searching for answers.
Maybe you're searching for yourself.
Maybe you don't yet have the words for what you're going through.

That's okay.
This book is for you.

Take what you need from these pages.
Leave what doesn't fit.
But know this:
Your story matters.
Your future matters.
And no matter where you're starting from, change is possible — even if you can't see it yet.

Thank you for walking this journey with me.

With respect and hope,
Roman Sewell

FOUNDING REFORMED EAST SUSSEX

Reformed East Sussex was not born from a business plan or a moment of inspiration. It wasn't something I dreamed of in childhood or even imagined in the early years of my recovery. It came from something much simpler — the understanding that people like me were falling through the cracks, and no one was reaching out a hand.

After my time at Eco-Actif, after discovering purpose through helping others rebuild their lives, I began to see clearly how much support was missing in East Sussex. I saw people leaving prison with nowhere to go, no guidance, no stability, and no belief in themselves. I saw myself in them — the fear, the uncertainty, the weight of trying to re-enter a world that does not forgive easily.

I knew what it felt like to walk out of a prison gate and step straight into silence.
I knew what it felt like to be judged by a past I could not change.
I knew the danger of having no structure, no support, no hope.

And so Reformed East Sussex began — not as an organisation, but as a promise.
A promise that no one would have to walk that road alone.
A promise that people deserve second chances, third chances, however many it takes.
A promise that change is possible when someone believes in you.

The first office was nothing more than a desk and a laptop in a small room.
No fancy branding, no funding, no support network.
Just determination, lived experience, and a refusal to let people drown in the same silence I once faced.

From that tiny beginning came something far bigger than I ever expected.
Reformed became a lifeline — not just for the people who walked through our doors, but for me. It gave me purpose, direction, and a sense of identity I'd never had. It taught me leadership, compassion,

patience, and the power of showing up every day even when life feels heavy.

It grew because people needed it.
It grew because the system wasn't enough.
It grew because hope, once shared, becomes contagious.

Reformed East Sussex stands today not because I built it alone, but because of every person who believed in it, every life that changed through it, and every story that began anew inside its walls.

It is more than an organisation.
It is a community.
A message.
A movement.
A testament to what can happen when someone decides that their past will not decide their future.

And it exists because people once believed in me — Eco-Actif, my family, my friends — long before I truly understood who I was.

PROLOGUE — The Moment Everything Shifted

There wasn't one single moment that changed my life.
No dramatic scene, no sudden clarity, no lightning-bolt realisation.
My life shifted in quiet ways, over years of surviving, searching, and trying to make sense of a world that never seemed designed for someone like me.

But if I had to choose a moment—the one that stands out when I look back—it was the morning I woke up and felt an ache in my chest that I couldn't ignore. Not sadness. Not fear. Something deeper. Something honest.

It was the first time I admitted to myself that the life I was living did not belong to me.

That morning, I looked around the room, at the small details of the life I had built—relationships, routines, roles—and realised none of them felt like home. I had spent so long fighting to survive that I had forgotten what it meant to belong to myself.

That feeling led me here.
To rebuilding.
To truth.
To becoming.
This book is the story of how I got back to myself.

EPILOGUE — Becoming Whole

I used to think becoming whole meant fixing everything that was broken.
Now I understand that wholeness has nothing to do with perfection.
It's about alignment.
It's about truth.
It's about standing in your own skin—even if it took you years to arrive there.

I am not the person I used to be.
I am not the person the world tried to shape.
I am not the versions of myself that were created to survive hardship, judgement, or fear.

I am myself.
Finally.

And the journey continues—not as a struggle, but as a life I have chosen with intention.
A life where I help others rise.
A life where I live in my truth.
A life where I refuse to shrink for anyone.

If this book has taught you anything, I hope it's this:
You are allowed to become who you truly are.
No matter where you started.
No matter what you've been through.
No matter who told you otherwise.

The story doesn't end here.
Neither does yours.

Printed in the United Kingdom.
First edition.

ISBN: 978 -1-0369-7447-3
Contact: roman.sewell1@gmail.com

To those walking their own path of change and hope, may these words remind you that transformation is always possible.

A MESSAGE TO SURVIVORS

To everyone who has lived through things that should have broken you —
I see you.

Survival is not weakness.
Survival is strength in its purest form.

Your story does not need to be neat, tidy, or understandable to anyone else.
It only needs to be yours.

You are allowed to grow.
You are allowed to heal.
You are allowed to take up space in a world that once tried to erase you.

You deserve a life that feels like your own.
You deserve peace.
You deserve to live.

A MESSAGE TO PEOPLE LEAVING PRISON

You might feel lost.
You might feel judged.
You might feel like the world doesn't want you back.

I know those feelings well.

But listen to me when I say this:
Your past does not decide your future.
You do.

You are not the worst thing you have ever done.
You are not your mistakes.
You are not your sentence.

You are a person capable of rebuilding, capable of transformation, capable of becoming someone you are proud of.

Second chances exist.
Third chances exist.
As many chances as it takes — they exist.

Hold on.
Keep moving.
You matter.

A MESSAGE TO ANYONE QUESTIONING THEIR IDENTITY

You don't need permission to be yourself.
You don't need approval to exist.
You don't need to explain your truth to anyone who refuses to listen.

Your identity is yours — not a debate, not a negotiation, not a test.

If you feel different inside, trust that feeling.
If you feel unseen, understand you are not alone.
If you feel lost, know that many of us started exactly where you are now.

You deserve a life where your reflection matches who you are.
You deserve honesty, alignment, and peace.

You deserve to become yourself.

Transitioning wasn't an escape — it was a return.
A return to a truth I had buried under years of silence.
A return to a self I had been separated from since childhood.
A return to a body that finally felt like home.

Transitioning wasn't easy.
It wasn't neat.
It wasn't magical.
But it was necessary.

There were days of doubt.
Nights of fear.
Moments where old wounds reopened.
Times when the world felt louder than my courage.

But there were also moments of peace —
the first time I recognised myself,
the first time I breathed without hiding,
the first time I stood in the mirror and saw not confusion but clarity.

Transition is not about changing who you are.
It's about letting yourself exist.
It's about stepping into your own skin.
It's about living in truth, even when the world struggles to understand.

I did not become someone new.
I became who I always was.

Chapter X — The Transition Journey

Transitioning is often spoken about as if it is a single moment — a decision, a declaration, a switch from one life into another. But the truth is far more complex. Transition is not a beginning or an ending. It is an unfolding. A returning. A remembering of the self you were always meant to be.

For me, the journey began long before I ever said the words out loud.
It began in childhood, in those quiet moments when something felt "off," though I didn't yet have the language for it. I just knew the world saw me one way, and I felt another.

Early Feelings — The Unseen Battle

Growing up, I carried something heavy and invisible.
Every mirror felt like a reminder that the world expected me to perform a role I didn't recognise. Every photo put a lump in my throat. Every "she" felt like a scratch against my skin.

I didn't know what to call it.
I just knew I felt wrong — like I had been placed into a life that wasn't mine.

Learning to Hide

So, like many of us do, I hid it.
I pushed the truth so far down that I convinced myself it wasn't there.
I became a master at surviving — surviving expectations, surviving roles, surviving a world that didn't leave room for who I really was.

When life took me down difficult paths — homelessness, addiction, prison — my identity became something I couldn't even afford to think about. Survival leaves no space for self-discovery.

The Awakening

It wasn't until years later, in Eastbourne, in a life that finally looked stable, that the truth resurfaced. I had love. I had calm. I had a future. But inside, something was still painfully misaligned.

The reflection in the mirror still wasn't mine.

The truth returned, quiet at first, then louder, until it filled every corner of my being.
I could not keep pretending.

Leaving the life I had built — leaving the woman I loved — was the hardest decision I ever made. But it was the moment I chose survival of the *soul*, not survival of the *surface.*

Starting Hormone Therapy

The first appointment was terrifying.
Not because I doubted my identity — but because I feared the world's response to it.
But the moment testosterone entered my body, it felt like breathing after years underwater.

Changes came slowly, then all at once:

- My voice deepened.
- My jawline sharpened.
- My reflection finally started to align with my truth.
- The world's "she" became "he."
- And inside me, the war quieted.

The Emotional Journey

Transition is not just physical.
It is emotional, psychological, spiritual.

I shed layers of shame I didn't know I was carrying.
I grieved the years I lived as someone I was not.

I confronted the pain of memories where my identity was never recognised.

And I learned something important:
Transition does not erase your past — it frees you from being trapped in it.

Living as Myself

There is a peace in my life now that I never thought possible.
A stillness in my chest where chaos used to live.
A sense of alignment that no amount of pretending could ever offer.

Transition didn't make me someone new.
Transition allowed me to become myself.

The Message Behind My Journey

If my journey teaches anything, it's this:

You are allowed to exist.
You are allowed to change.
You are allowed to grow into the person you have always been.

This chapter is not the end of my transition.
It is the beginning of living — truly living — for the first time.

Prison is not just a place.
It is a world within a world — one where time slows, noise grows, and identity becomes something you tuck away to survive.

Inside, you learn quickly:
don't show weakness,
don't show fear,
don't show yourself.

I survived by becoming smaller, harder, quieter.
Every day was a battle between who I was and who I needed to be to make it out alive.

Recovery didn't begin in prison —
but prison planted the seed.

It made me realise that if I didn't change something,
I would die in the same cycle I was born into.

Recovery was brutal.
It was honesty.
It was accountability.
It was choosing a new path every single day.
Some days I walked it.
Some days I crawled.

Identity came later —
after the noise quieted,
after the chaos eased,
after I finally had space to hear myself.

And when I did, the truth was waiting:

I was not the person the world thought I was.
I was not the person I forced myself to be.
I was not a statistic, a label, or a record.

I was me.
And I was finally ready to become who I was meant to be.

CHAPTER X — The Years in the Shadows: Brothels and the Streets

People imagine that sex work is a straight road — that you walk into it by choice, by desire, by some kind of reckless impulse.
But that's not how it happens for most of us.

For many, it begins in the cracks of life — the places where safety doesn't exist, where survival becomes the only goal, where you're choosing between hunger and harm, homelessness and danger, loneliness and exploitation.

My path didn't start in a brothel.
It started long before that —
in instability,
in trauma,
in homelessness,
in moments where the world felt cold and indifferent.

And when you have no home, no money, no support, and no belief that your life is worth more than your circumstances, the streets become your teacher.

The Streets — The First Step Into Survival

The streets weren't a place you "went to."
They were a place you ended up.

Nights were long and cold.
People passed by without seeing you.
Sometimes, the only people who recognised your existence were those who wanted something from you — or wanted to hurt you.

But the streets also had their own kind of community.
People who had lost everything shared cigarettes, blankets, warnings, food, and advice.
We weren't friends.
We were survivors.
And survivors stick together.

The streets were dangerous, yes — but they were also honest.
People there didn't hide who they were.
They couldn't afford to.

And that's where I first learned the rule:

When you have nothing left, your body becomes the last currency the world recognises.

How the Streets Led to Brothels

The shift from the streets to brothels wasn't a decision.
It was a pull — gradual, quiet, and wrapped in promises that sounded better than freezing corners and unsafe nights.

Brothels offered:

- A roof
- A warm room
- Some protection
- Money that didn't disappear
- A place to rest
- A moment to breathe

When you're living day to day, that sounds like salvation.

But brothels had their own world —
unspoken rules,
a hierarchy,
faces hardened by years of surviving,
and people doing whatever they needed to do to stay alive.

People judge brothels harshly.
But the truth is, many people there were like me —
not criminals, not villains, not immoral —
just exhausted, desperate humans trying to make it through another day.

Two Different Worlds, One Battle

The streets were unpredictable.
The brothels were controlled.

But both demanded the same thing:
disconnect from who you are.

Working on the streets meant risking violence, judgement, and danger.
Working in brothels meant giving up parts of yourself just to keep going.

Either way, survival came at a cost.

Identity Buried Under Survival

During those years — both in the brothels and on the streets — my identity was something I kept buried deeper than anything else.

I didn't feel like the person people saw.
I didn't feel connected to the role the world placed me in.
I felt trapped inside a body and a life that never aligned with my truth.

When you're already hiding to stay alive, hiding yourself becomes automatic.

In the brothels, I often felt like I was watching my own life from outside my body — a silent witness to things I never truly wanted, living a script I never wrote.

The disconnect was suffocating.

The People I Met

Despite everything, I met some of the strongest people in those years:

- Women who were running from violence
- Young people rejected by their families
- People fighting addiction
- People fighting poverty
- People fighting themselves
- People who had nowhere else to go

We protected each other.
We shared warnings, food, stories.
We sat together in the quiet hours when the world outside kept moving, forgetting we existed.

I saw more kindness in broken places than I ever saw in polished ones.

Leaving That World Behind

Leaving wasn't a single day.
It was a series of moments:

- The moment I realised I wanted more.
- The moment I realised I deserved more.
- The moment I realised survival wasn't enough anymore.

It took courage I didn't know I had.
It took strength I didn't believe was mine.
It took walking away from the only stability I'd known.

I left with nothing but a determination that my life had to change — even if I didn't know how yet.

What Those Years Taught Me

The streets taught me resilience.
The brothels taught me compassion.
Both taught me that people are not defined by the darkest places they end up in.

Most importantly, those years taught me this:

Survival is not shameful.
What you do to stay alive does not define your worth.

I carried those lessons with me into every chapter that followed —
through recovery,
through rebuilding,
through founding Reformed East Sussex,
through discovering my identity,
through transitioning,
through becoming the man I am now.

Those years were painful.
But they were also part of my becoming.

And I survived them.

Chapter X — Letters to My Younger Self

To the child who didn't feel right in their own skin:

You're not broken.
You're not confused.
You're not wrong.
You're just early.

The world won't always understand you, but one day *you* will — and that will be enough.

To the teenager trying to disappear:

You don't have to be strong all the time.
Crying does not make you weak.
Silence does not protect you.
You're allowed to want more.
Your life will not always feel this heavy.

To the young adult lost in survival mode:

You are not your mistakes.
You are not your circumstances.
You are not the names they called you.
You will rise.
You will rebuild.
You will transform.

To the person walking out of prison with fear in their chest:

Your story is not over.
You will find purpose.
You will find direction.
You will help others in ways you cannot yet imagine.

To the version of you who hid your identity:

I forgive you.
You did what you had to do to survive.
But one day, you will no longer need to hide.
One day, you will become yourself.
And it will be worth every struggle.

To the person you are becoming:

Keep going.
Keep growing.
Keep choosing yourself.
You will stand in the sun again.

Chapter X — A Message to Men

To the men who are hurting in silence,
To the men who feel they can't speak,
To the men carrying their weight alone,
To the men discovering who they are —
this is for you.

Strength is not silence.
Strength is not suppression.
Strength is not dying a little inside every day just to fit in.

Real strength is honesty.
Real strength is vulnerability.
Real strength is saying, "This is who I am," even when your voice shakes.

To trans men especially:
You are valid.
You are real.
You belong.
Your manhood is not defined by others — it is defined by you.

Walk tall.

Chapter X — A Message to the LGBTQ+ Community

To my community —
thank you.

Thank you for existing in a world that wasn't built for us.
Thank you for surviving.
Thank you for fighting for rights we should have always had.
Thank you for making space for people like me.

You taught me that identity is not shameful.
You taught me that truth is worth the struggle.
You taught me that chosen family is sometimes the strongest family there is.

To every trans person reading this:
You are not a phase.
You are not a confusion.
You are not "too much."
You are a human being deserving of dignity, love, and respect.

Your existence is revolutionary.
Never forget that.

GLOSSARY OF TERMS

Glossary

Transition:
The process of aligning your external identity with your internal truth.

Gender Dysphoria:
Emotional distress caused by a mismatch between one's assigned sex and true gender identity.

Testosterone (HRT):
Hormone therapy used by many trans men.

Deadname:
A name assigned at birth that no longer represents a trans person.

Rehabilitation:
The process of rebuilding life after prison, addiction, or trauma.

Reformed East Sussex:
A support service founded by Roman Sewell to help people rebuild their lives.

Lived Experience:
Knowledge gained through personal hardship, not textbooks.

RESOURCES PAGE

Where to Get Help

Mental Health Support:
Samaritans — 116 123
Mind UK — mind.org.uk

LGBTQ+ Support:
Stonewall — stonewall.org.uk
Mermaids UK — mermaidsuk.org.uk
Switchboard LGBT+ Helpline — 0300 330 0630

Transition Support:
Gender Identity Clinics (NHS)
TransActual — transactual.org.uk

Prison & Rehabilitation Support:
Nacro — nacro.org.uk
Unlock — unlock.org.uk

Addiction Recovery:
AA, NA, SMART Recovery
Local support hubs

Emergency Help:
If in crisis, contact your local emergency number.

A Page of Famous Quotes

"Out of difficulties grow miracles."
— *Jean de La Bruyère*

"It is never too late to be what you might have been."
— *George Eliot*

"In the middle of every difficulty lies opportunity."
— *Albert Einstein*

"The only journey is the one within."
— *Rainer Maria Rilke*

"What lies behind us and what lies before us are tiny matters compared to what lies within us."
— *Ralph Waldo Emerson*

"The wound is the place where the light enters you."
— *Rumi*

"Fall seven times, stand up eight."
— *Japanese Proverb*

"Courage is not the absence of fear, but the triumph over it."
— *Nelson Mandela*

"You either walk inside your story and own it, or you stand outside your story and hustle for your worthiness."
— *Brené Brown*

"Your past is just a story. And once you realise this, it has no power over you."
— *Chuck Palahniuk*

"Hardships often prepare ordinary people for an extraordinary destiny."
— *C.S. Lewis*

"You must do the thing you think you cannot do."
— *Eleanor Roosevelt*

"There is no greater agony than bearing an untold story inside you."
— *Maya Angelou*

"We are all broken, that's how the light gets in."
— *Leonard Cohen*

"The greatest glory in living lies not in never falling, but in rising every time we fall."
— *Nelson Mandela*

"You cannot swim for new horizons until you have courage to lose sight of the shore."
— *William Faulkner*

"I am not what happened to me, I am what I choose to become."
— *Carl Jung*

"You never know how strong you are until being strong is your only choice."
— *Bob Marley*

"Although the world is full of suffering, it is also full of the overcoming of it."
— *Helen Keller*

"Rock bottom became the solid foundation on which I rebuilt my life."
— *J.K. Rowling*

"Do not judge me by my success, judge me by how many times I fell down and got back up again."
— *Nelson Mandela*

"We must embrace pain and burn it as fuel for our journey."
— *Kenji Miyazawa*

"Patience and fortitude conquer all things."
— *Ralph Waldo Emerson*

"Strength grows in the moments when you think you cannot go on, but you keep going anyway."
— *Unknown*

Quotes on Identity & Becoming Yourself

"To be yourself in a world that is constantly trying to make you something else is the greatest accomplishment."
— *Ralph Waldo Emerson*

"The privilege of a lifetime is to become who you truly are."
— *Carl Jung*

"Your life is yours to create. Don't ever let anyone make you feel like you don't deserve to be who you are."
— *Unknown*

"The most courageous act is still to think for yourself. Aloud."
— *Coco Chanel*

"You either live with the pain of being untrue to yourself, or the pain of growing into who you are meant to be."
— *Unknown*

"We are not what the world makes us. We are what we make of ourselves."
— *Sartre*

"Owning our story and loving ourselves through that process is the bravest thing we'll ever do."
— *Brené Brown*

"Your true self is who you are when no one is watching."
— *Unknown*

"Hope is being able to see that there is light despite all of the darkness."
— *Desmond Tutu*

"No matter how hard the past, you can always begin again."
— *Buddha*

"Healing is not linear."
— *Unknown*

"Just when the caterpillar thought the world was over, it became a butterfly."
— *Proverb*

"Turn your wounds into wisdom."
— *Oprah Winfrey*

"Every saint has a past, and every sinner has a future."
— *Oscar Wilde*

"The comeback is always stronger than the setback."
— *Unknown*

"Sometimes the smallest step in the right direction ends up being the biggest step of your life."
— *Unknown*

"The darkest nights produce the brightest stars."
— *John Green*

A Note to the Reader

Before you begin this book, I want to tell you something from the heart.

This story is raw. It is painful in places. It is honest in ways that may surprise you. But it is also a story of survival, hope, and transformation — proof that even the darkest chapters can lead to light.

I am not sharing these pages for sympathy. I am sharing them because somewhere out there, someone feels lost, broken, or alone, and needs to know that they are not beyond saving.

Every memory in this book was lived by a younger version of me — a scared child, a lost teenager, a hurting young adult who didn't know how to ask for help. As you read, I ask you to remember that healing takes time, and sometimes the hardest part is admitting that we deserve it.

There were moments in my life when I didn't think I would make it. Moments when hope felt out of reach. Moments when I couldn't see a future for myself at all.

But I'm still here. And so are you.

If my story does anything, I hope it reminds you that strength doesn't always look like bravery. Sometimes it looks like surviving one more day. Sometimes it looks like getting back up after life has knocked you down over and over again. And sometimes it looks like simply choosing to keep going.

Thank you for being here — for turning these pages, for walking this journey with me, and for giving my story a place in your hands and your heart.

I hope that somewhere within these chapters, you find a piece of your own strength reflected back at you.

With gratitude, Roman Sewell

Chapter 1

Shadows of Childhood

My earliest memories are of a home that stopped feeling safe far too soon.

After my dad died — lost to addiction — our family began to fall apart. The grief was unbearable, and into that space came a man who would bring years of fear and pain. My

stepfather's anger controlled the house; every sound, every shadow could mean trouble.

There were nights that felt endless — nights where I became the shield between my stepdad and the rest of the house. I was only eleven, but somehow I understood that if I stayed awake with him, if I sat there pretending everything was fine, maybe he wouldn't storm into the bedroom where my mum and sister were hiding.

I remember those nights far too clearly. Him slumped in a chair, drink in hand, swaying, muttering, sometimes shouting at shadows only he could see. The smell of alcohol was heavy in the air, mixing with the sharp fear that always lived in my stomach. I'd sit across from him, tired and scared, pretending not to flinch every time he raised his voice or slammed something down.

They were long nights — painfully long. My child's body wanted to sleep, but my mind wouldn't let me. I felt like it was my responsibility to keep the peace, to keep him occupied, to keep him away from the people I loved most. No child should ever have to sit up through the night to protect their family from a grown man, but I did. I didn't know any different.

And then there were the times he'd take me out with him — drunk, angry, unpredictable. He'd drag me into the car, the smell of beer and tobacco thick in the air, and drive us to pubs where he'd drink even more. I remember sitting in those places feeling small, embarrassed, humiliated. I'd watch other people looking at him, at us, and I knew what they must have been thinking:

2

Who brings a child into a pub like this? Why is he so drunk? What kind of life does that kid have?

Even at eleven, shame crept into my bones. I hated the way he slurred my name. I hated the way people stared. I hated that I couldn't escape.

But what I hated most was knowing I'd have to go home with him
— sit up again, watch him stumble around the house, and do everything in my power to stop him from waking my mum and sister. I took on a role no child should ever have — protector, peacekeeper, barrier between them and the storm.

I didn't realise it then, but those nights shaped me. They taught me how to read danger. How to stay quiet. How to endure. How to survive.

And they taught me something else — something I would only understand years later: I wasn't weak for being afraid. I was strong for surviving him.

There was a moment when I was eleven that I've never forgotten — a moment where the sadness inside me felt too big for my young mind to understand. Life at home was chaotic, fear lived in the walls, and I felt completely alone. One night, the weight of everything became too much. I tried to escape the pain in a way no child should ever feel driven to, but instead I ended up on the floor of my bedroom, shaken and confused.

I remember sitting there, my heart racing, staring at the curtains and the quiet shadows on the wall. I didn't cry. I didn't shout. I just felt empty — the kind of emptiness that makes the air feel colder than it should. I didn't understand why I was still there, why I was meant to keep going, or what the next day would even look like.

And I never told my mum. Not because I didn't want to. But because deep down, I knew she was fighting her own battles — battles too heavy for me to add to. She was barely holding herself together, and I was terrified that knowing how close I had come to giving up would break her completely. So I carried that moment alone, a secret I tucked away inside myself for years.

Looking back, I see that I wasn't weak — I was a child trying to

3

survive a world that felt far too dark. And somehow, even in that moment, life kept me here. Maybe it was a chance. Maybe it was

4

something bigger. But it was the first quiet sign that my story wasn't over yet.

Growing up like that changes you. You learn to read people's moods before they speak. You learn silence. You learn to survive.

My mum tried to keep us safe, but the violence got worse. I remember nights of running, the echo of doors slamming behind us, clutching my sister's hand as we fled to women's refuges.

We'd arrive with nothing but a small bag and hope that maybe this time, we could start again.

"Out of suffering have emerged the strongest souls; the most massive characters are seared with scars."

Kahlil Gibran

5

6

Chapter 2

Lost and Found

By the time I reached my teenage years, I'd already seen too much of life.

Fear had become normal. Chaos was familiar. When you grow up in constant survival mode, it's hard to know what peace even feels like.

After we ran away from my stepdad, the refuges were small, cramped, and always full of people trying to piece together lives that had been broken by violence. But despite the fear, despite the constant uncertainty, there was also a strange kind of safety in those places. A sense that at least the danger was outside, not inside.

Some nights, I remember lying on those thin mattresses, listening to whispers in the hallways — women crying quietly, kids trying to sleep through the nightmares that followed them everywhere. In those places, you learned to recognise the sound of someone else's pain because it matched your own.

There were nights in the refuges that still stay with me. Nights when the building felt too quiet, as if everyone was holding their breath at the same time. My mum would sometimes lock herself in the small bathroom, and I'd sit outside the door pretending I wasn't listening. But I could hear her — the soft, painful sound of her trying not to cry. It wasn't loud; it was a quiet whimper, the kind that breaks you more than screams ever could. I remember staring at the floor, wishing I could make it stop, wishing I could take away her pain. But I was just a kid, clutching my sister's hand, trying to be brave while the person who was supposed to protect us was breaking in the next room. Those nights taught me that adults can hurt too, and that sometimes the strongest people are the ones crying silently behind a locked door.

Back then, I didn't understand. I just knew it scared me. I knew I hated hearing her pain.

7

My sister and I would sit together in the dim hallway light, not speaking, not crying, just holding onto each other while Mum broke

 8

down two feet away.

It's only now I realise she did try. She tried with everything she had left. But she was broken — worn down by fear, by love, by violence, by the impossible choices she was forced to make. She was fighting battles I was too young to see, holding us together with hands that were trembling the whole time.

I used to think she failed us. Now I see she was surviving the best way she could.

For a while, I believed that maybe this new life — even with all its instability — would be a fresh start.

But life has a cruel way of circling back might finally settle. But it didn't and somewhere in between, I started to fall apart inside.

When my mum went back to him, everything inside me shattered. I didn't just lose hope — I lost trust. I remember the exact moment it happened, the moment the world as I knew it disappeared.

He was sitting on the sofa when I walked in, his arm draped over the back as if he'd never hurt us, never threatened us, never forced us out of our home. He looked at me with this smug, cold stare, and something inside me snapped. It wasn't anger. It was something deeper — a feeling that the world wasn't safe, that adults weren't safe, that love couldn't be trusted.

I felt abandoned by the one person who was supposed to protect me. I felt invisible.

After that, everything spiralled quickly. I was drowning inside myself, and the only thing I knew how to do was numb the pain. Self-harm became a release, a way to feel something other than emptiness. Inhaling things, drinking, anything that blurred the edges of my thoughts — it was never about wanting to die, not at first. It was about wanting the pain to stop, even for a moment.

One day, when I was fourteen, my mum walked in and caught me cutting myself. The look on her face wasn't just shock — it was fear. Fear of what I'd become, fear of what she didn't know how to stop. That moment changed everything. She told me my

9

aunt was coming to pick me up, that I couldn't stay there anymore.

I packed a bag in silence.

I didn't cry. I didn't argue. I just left.

10

At first, living with my aunt felt like a chance — like maybe I could turn things around. She tried, she really did. She set rules, boundaries, and tried to show me what stability looked like. But I was already too far gone, too angry, too lost. I was a storm she didn't know how to contain.

By my fifteenth birthday, the cracks had deepened. I had started drinking heavily, skipping school, disappearing for days at a time. I didn't care about my future because I didn't believe I had one. The day she told me I had to leave, she cried — but I didn't. I just picked up my things and walked out into a world that felt cold and familiar.

And just like that, I was homeless.

At first, I bounced between friends' sofas — always careful not to overstay, always pretending I was fine. But those couches weren't homes, and deep down I knew it. The days blurred into nights, the nights blurred into more nights, and survival became my full-time job.

I slept in hostels when they had space. When they didn't, I slept in parks. Some nights were freezing; some were terrifying. You learn to sleep with one ear open, to hide your belongings under your clothes, to trust no one completely.

And then came the streets — the dark corners, the whispered exchanges, the things you do when you have nowhere else to go.

That's when I first started selling my body.

People have a lot of opinions about that, but they never ask about the circumstances. They never ask about the fear, the hunger, the cold, the loneliness, the hopelessness. They never ask what it feels like to be fifteen and watched by men twice your age who see you as nothing more than a transaction.

It wasn't a choice. Not really.

It was survival.

The Gypsy Girl and Her Family

When I was homeless, drifting from one place to another with no real direction, I met a gypsy girl who was around my age —

11

sixteen, maybe seventeen. There was something about her that felt different from anyone I'd met. She had this confidence, this spark, this way of carrying herself like the world couldn't touch her. She was a beautiful human being and I'm in no doubt she still is.

12

Her family welcomed me when I had nowhere else to go some nights. They didn't judge me. They opened their door, their home, and their arms to a complete stranger because they could see how lost I was.

They clothed me. They fed me. They gave me somewhere to sleep that wasn't cold, dangerous, or temporary.

Looking back, I know they felt sorry for me — this skinny, smelly broken kid who didn't have a home, who didn't even know what tomorrow would look like. But their kindness wasn't pity. It was compassion — something I hadn't felt in a long time.

They treated me like a human being, when the world had been treating me like an afterthought.

I will always be grateful for them. For their warmth. For their food.

For the clothing they offered without hesitation. For seeing a scared young person and choosing to care.

Their kindness didn't fix my life — but it reminded me that not everyone in the world was dangerous. Not everyone wanted something from me. Not everyone would turn their back. Sometimes, people just cared. And at a time when I had nothing, that meant everything.

The streets became their own world, one with its own rules and dangers. I learned how to read people fast — who might hurt me, who might help me, who might pretend to care but only wanted something in return. I learned how to fake confidence, how to smile when inside I felt like I was disappearing.

The days were blurry, and the nights were even worse. I drank to forget. I used to disappear. I put on a mask every day because pretending was easier than trying to explain a pain no one wanted to hear.

Looking back now, I see a scared child trying desperately to find something — stability, safety, belonging, anything. But back then, all I saw was darkness. All I felt was emptiness.

And then… something shifted.

It didn't happen in a dramatic moment. It didn't come with

13

bright lights or a sudden awakening. It came quietly, almost too softly to notice — a small, fragile spark of hope.

14

Maybe it was a person. Maybe a moment. Maybe just the simple thought that life didn't have to stay this way.

I didn't know it then, but those tiny moments — the ones you barely recognise at the time — are sometimes the ones that save you.

"It takes courage to grow up and become who you really are."
E.E. Cummings

15

Chapter 3

Behind Prison Walls

I was lost and not found. I hated this world; I hated everyone. By the time I reached my late teens, the world felt like a place I didn't belong in — a place I watched from the outside, hollowed out by years of chaos, hurt, and survival. I hated the world. I hated people. But mostly, I hated myself.

The years became a blur of park benches, strangers' sofas, dingy hostels, and cold waiting rooms where the lights buzzed too loudly and the chairs hurt your back. There were too many police cells to count — the kind where time doesn't exist and the walls feel like they're closing in. And then there were the hospitals, where I'd be admitted over and over "for my own safety." They patched up my body, but no one knew how to reach my mind.

I wasn't living. I was drifting — from crisis to crisis, from night to night.

The Murder Charge - Old Baily

One of the darkest and most terrifying moments of my life was when I was put on a murder charge. Even now, saying the words feels surreal, like I'm talking about someone else. But it was real — painfully real.

The secure unit was unlike anything I had ever experienced. The moment the door slammed behind me, the sound echoed so deeply through my chest that I felt it in my bones. I was the only female there
— a terrified teenager surrounded by men who had been labelled with the darkest crimes imaginable. Rapists. Murderers. Even people who the staff whispered about in ways that made my stomach drop.

I remember standing in that corridor, the fluorescent lights buzzing overhead, and realising I had been placed in a world completely cut off from anything familiar. I didn't belong there, yet somehow, there I was

16

— the only girl among people whose crimes were the kind I had only ever heard about on the news.

I was so scared. Not just of them, but of the entire environment — the shouting, the unpredictability, the way the air felt heavy with

17

tension. I barely slept. I barely breathed. Every sound made me jump. Every footstep in the hall made my heart pound. I tried to make myself small, invisible, hoping no one would notice me.

But fear noticed me. Loneliness noticed me.

It was a place where time didn't move normally, where nights stretched on endlessly and mornings arrived without comfort. I felt trapped in a nightmare I couldn't wake up from, surrounded by people whose realities were worlds apart from mine. I was young, broken, overwhelmed — and completely out of my depth.

Looking back, I don't know how I survived those months. But I did. And surviving that place taught me something I would only understand years later: I had a strength inside me that no one had ever told me I had.

The air inside felt thick, electric, unpredictable. Some men screamed in the shadows. Some stared into the distance, lost to a world only they could see. Some banged on the walls until their hands bled.

I wasn't sure which one of them I would become.

Nights there were the worst — lying awake, listening to screams ricochet down the corridor, wondering if I'd ever get out alive, or sane. I'd close my eyes and see flashes of my childhood, my mum, the girl I used to be before everything fell apart. And then I'd open them again to the harsh, artificial light and remember where I really was.

That place broke something in me. But strangely, it also made something else wake up.

That place changed me. It made me realise how close I was to never coming back.

When the case moved forward and I ended up in Holloway Prison, it felt like stepping into a different world — bleak, loud, and unforgiving. Holloway wasn't just a building with bars. It was its own universe, filled with women who carried stories the outside world didn't want to hear.

Some had lost everything. Some had never had anything to begin with. Some were fighters. Some were fragile. All of us were broken

18

in our own ways.

The prison officers' keys jingling down the corridors became the soundtrack of my days. The shouts, the arguments, the tears, the forced

19

laughter — they all mixed together until you couldn't tell where one story ended and another began.

At first, I kept my head down. I didn't trust anyone — not the officers, not the inmates, not myself.

But prison has a way of forcing you to see things, especially yourself.

The day the cell door closed behind me, the sound echoed through my chest.

It wasn't just the clang of metal — it was the sound of every bad choice, every scar, every scream I'd ever buried inside.

Prison was a place I'd promised myself I'd never end up, but somehow, I wasn't surprised to be there. When you live in survival mode long enough, the line between danger and normal disappears.

Holloway wasn't just a prison — it was a world within walls. Women from every kind of pain lived side by side: mothers, addicts, fighters, survivors. Each one of us carried stories that the world outside didn't want to hear.

The Night Everything Shifted

One night stands out more than any other.

The wing was loud as usual — shouting, banging, women calling to each other through doors. Then suddenly, the noise changed. I heard officers running, keys clattering, shouting breaking through the usual chaos.

Then silence. A heavy, suffocating silence.

And then it came — a scream so raw and full of grief that it carved itself into my memory forever. A woman had just lost her friend in the cell next to hers. Her friend had taken her own life.

That scream wasn't just pain. It was every unspoken fear, every buried trauma, every moment of hopelessness rolled into one long, agonising cry.

I lay there in my cell, frozen, listening. And something inside me cracked open.

For the first time in a long time, I realised I didn't want to die. I

20

didn't want to be another scream echoing down those cold halls.

But I also didn't know how to live.

21

While I was in Holloway, I found out I was pregnant. The news hit me like a wave — terrifying, confusing, and strangely hopeful. I had no idea what it meant for me, for the baby, for anything.

When the time came to give birth, they took me to the hospital. I remember the sterile smell, the harsh lights, the fear crawling up my throat. I folded tiny baby clothes, prepared a little cradle. For a moment, I allowed myself to imagine holding her.

But life didn't work like that for me back then.

As soon as she was born — literally seconds after — three people rushed in. My legs were still open. My heart was still racing. I hadn't even seen her properly.

They took her. Just like that. No goodbye. No moment. No chance.

I sat on that cold metal bed afterward, staring at the wall, numb. I didn't scream. I didn't cry at first. I was empty — a teenager who had lost a child in the most brutal, detached way possible.

Looking back, I understand why. My life was chaotic. I wasn't ready. I had nothing to give. But at the time… the pain was unbearable.

I was just a teenager — lost, angry, broken and on a murder charge

.

When I was finally released, they handed me a travel card and a small bag — that was it. No plan, no home, no direction. The world outside looked exactly the same as it had before, but something in me had changed.

I was terrified of freedom. I was terrified of myself.

But I was also holding onto something tiny — something I hadn't felt in a long time.

Hope. Not much. Just a spark.

But sometimes, a spark is enough to start a fire.

22

"Even in the darkest place, a spark of hope can survive."
— Unknown

 23

Chapter 4

Recovery and Rebuilding

Coming out of prison, freedom felt strange — almost unreal. For so long, my life had been ruled by locked doors, strict routines, and other people deciding when I could eat, sleep, or breathe. When those gates finally opened, I stepped out feeling like a stranger in the world. I had a travel card in my hand, a plastic bag with barely anything inside, and a heart full of fear.

The air felt different. The sky looked too big. The noise of the streets was overwhelming, like the world had kept moving without me and I was now trying to catch up.

I tried to walk confidently, but inside I was trembling. I didn't know where I belonged. I didn't know who I was outside those walls. For years, I had been defined by what I'd been through — the trauma, the mistakes, the chaos. But now, standing on the pavement with nowhere to go, I realised I had no idea how to start again.

I went from one temporary place to another — hostels, friends' sofas, emergency accommodation. Some nights were okay. Some nights weren't. I still carried so much pain, so much confusion, so much self-blame. And surviving your past is one thing… but learning to live after it is something else entirely.

"Something has to change."

There came a moment — quiet, but powerful — when I realised I couldn't keep living in the same cycle. I was tired. Tired of running from myself. Tired of hurting. Tired of pretending I didn't care.

Something inside me whispered:

If you don't change something now… you're not going to survive this.

It wasn't some dramatic revelation. It was just a tired truth. A small voice that refused to go silent this time.

I was in my early twenties when I found out I was pregnant again. And for a brief moment, I thought maybe this was it —

24

maybe this was my chance to build a different kind of life. My son was born, and he was beautiful. I loved him with a fierce, confused, overwhelming love

25

I didn't know how to describe.

But love alone doesn't undo years of trauma. Love doesn't magically give you stability. Love doesn't heal wounds you've never confronted.

As much as it destroyed me to admit it, I wasn't ready to be the mother he deserved. My life was still chaotic. I didn't want him to grow up the way I did — scared, unstable, constantly on edge.

So with my ex, we made a decision that broke me in ways I can still feel today. He went to live with her.

Letting him go wasn't giving up. It was loving him enough to put him first.

But that decision left a hole in me. I carried that loss like a shadow everywhere I went — and in a strange way, it also pushed me to start rebuilding my life. I wanted to become someone he could one day be proud of. Someone who had survived, changed, and risen again.

Tiny steps

Recovery didn't come all at once. It didn't come with big breakthroughs or grand moments of clarity. It came in tiny decisions — the kind no one else sees.

Waking up and deciding not to drink that day. Choosing to show up to appointments. Learning how to trust people again, slowly, painfully. Learning how to trust myself.

There were setbacks — plenty of them. Days when I fell apart, when the past swallowed me whole, when the guilt was so heavy I could barely breathe. But there were also days when something small went right. Days when I felt stronger, even if only a little.

I learned that recovery isn't a straight line. It's a messy, painful, beautiful climb — full of slips, stumbles, and tiny victories.

Finding Purpose

I started looking for ways to build something stable.

Volunteering.

Attending programs. Finding support services that understood people who'd been through the system. It wasn't easy. I was still

26

guarded, still expecting judgement, still terrified someone would look at my past and decide I wasn't worth helping.

But slowly, I began to come across people who didn't see me as a lost cause.

27

People who believed I could do more. People who treated me like I was human — not just a file, a mistake, or a statistic.

At first, I didn't believe them. But eventually, their belief started to crack through the walls I had built around myself.

I learned something important in those early days: You can rebuild your life, but you can't do it alone.

A New Strength

People often talk about healing like it's a soft, gentle process. But real healing — the kind that comes after years of trauma — is gritty. It's hard. It forces you to look at parts of yourself you've spent years avoiding.

I faced memories I'd buried. I confronted choices I'd blamed myself for. I learned to forgive myself, slowly, painfully.

I realised I wasn't weak for what I'd been through. I wasn't broken beyond repair. I had survived things that would have destroyed most people.

And somewhere along the way, survival turned into strength.

A Quote That Carried Me

"Even in the darkest night, the stars are still there — you just have to look up."

I used to think quotes like that were clichés. But there were nights when I clung to those words like a lifeline. Nights when it felt like the darkness would swallow me again.

And yet… I kept looking up.

I kept searching for those stars — even when they were hard to see.

Because every time I found one, even the tiniest glimmer of light, I was reminded of something important:

I was still here. I was still fighting. It was still possible.

28

29

I found myself in rooms with people who had walked similar roads — addiction, homelessness, prison, trauma. We spoke the same silent language, the one built on surviving things most people never see.

There was comfort in that. Not because I wanted to stay in the past, but because I felt understood.

The more I showed up, the more I began to feel something I hadn't felt in years: hope. Tiny, fragile, but real. I began to imagine a life where my past didn't define my future. A life where I wasn't just surviving — I was building something.

I started volunteering more. I helped out where I could. I showed up even on days when everything in me screamed not to. And bit by bit, I learned new skills — how to organise things, support others, talk to people, be part of a team.

For the first time, I wasn't running from my past. I was learning from it.

30

"Even in the darkest night, the stars are still there — you just have to look up."

Unknown

31

Chapter 5

Living the Truth

Freedom felt strange at first. After so many years of chaos, noise, locked doors, and people telling me who I was and where I could go, silence became unfamiliar. I would wake up some mornings expecting someone to shout my name, expecting the sound of keys, alarms, arguments in the hallways.

But instead, there was stillness. A quiet that felt heavy at first — almost threatening — because I didn't know how to exist without survival mode.

I was free, yes. But freedom doesn't magically heal you. I was still carrying years of shame, trauma, secrets, and memories that clung to me like a shadow. I didn't know how to live without looking over my shoulder. I didn't know how to trust myself, let alone other people.

For a while, I drifted between old habits and new hopes — caught somewhere between the person I had been and the person I wanted to become. Change didn't arrive in one clean moment. It came in waves

— messy, unpredictable, and sometimes overwhelming.

Searching for Myself

Those years after prison felt like a strange kind of in-between. I wasn't who I used to be, but I didn't yet know who I was becoming. I was unlearning everything that had kept me alive in the darkness — the emotional armour, the silence, the instinct to run, the need to disappear.

Some mornings, I'd wake up feeling strong. Other days, I felt like a child again — lost, confused, unsure of my place in the world. Healing isn't a straight line. It's a loop, a spiral, a climb that takes everything out of you.

Back then, I didn't realise just how brave it is to keep going when you don't know who you're trying to become.

There were nights when I'd lie awake replaying my whole life

32

— every moment of pain, every choice I regretted, every version of myself I'd had to bury just to survive. And slowly, I began to see a pattern:

33

Every broken piece of me had been trying to protect something — the real me, the truth I had never spoken, the self I had never allowed to breathe.

Those years changed me. They taught me how strong I really was, even when I didn't know it. I met people who were broken, lost, and beautiful in their own way. We were all just trying to make it through another day.

Looking back, I see that even in the darkest places, I was searching
— for belonging, for safety, for a reason to believe there was more to life than pain.

The Morning Everything Shifted

I remember the morning things started to truly change. It wasn't dramatic. There was no big sign. It was quiet — almost gentle.

I woke up feeling heavier than usual, like the weight of everything I'd been carrying had settled deeper in my chest overnight. The world outside was grey, the kind of sky that makes you feel like time is slowing down.

I made myself a cup of coffee and sat by the window, watching the light creep across the rooftops. For a long time, I just sat there, staring, my thoughts louder than the silence.

I kept asking myself:

Who am I? What am I doing? Why do I still feel like I'm pretending? Why does my reflection never feel like mine?

It was a moment of truth I could no longer push aside. My whole life, I had been hiding behind versions of myself — the tough one, the broken one, the angry one, the survivor, the one who kept going no matter what. But none of them felt like home.

Inside, I felt like someone else entirely. Someone I had always been but never dared to become.

Sitting there with a warm mug between my hands, I realised I couldn't keep living half a life. I couldn't keep fitting myself into a shape that wasn't mine.

34

That morning, something inside me whispered a truth I had always known:

You deserve to live as yourself.

35

Eco Actif and Finding Purpose

Not long after, someone told me about a service called Eco Actif. It was meant for people like me — people who had been through the system, people who needed a second chance, people who wanted to rebuild.

I didn't expect much. I was used to being judged, written off, dismissed before I even opened my mouth.

But when I walked through their doors, something felt different.

They didn't see a criminal. They didn't see an addict. They didn't see a lost cause.

They saw me — or at least, they tried to.

They listened. They encouraged me. They believed in me long before I believed in myself.

A staff member once said to me, "You have potential. You just haven't seen it yet."

Those words stayed with me.

I began volunteering. Showing up. Helping however I could. It wasn't glamorous — making tea, organising paperwork, helping others who had walked roads like mine — but it was meaningful. It gave me structure, purpose, a place to belong.

Slowly, confidence began to grow where shame had lived for so long.

When they encouraged me to apply for a full-time job, I felt sick with fear. Me? A real job? With responsibility? With people who trusted me?

But they believed in me. So I took a chance.

And when I got the job, I cried — not because I was overwhelmed, but because for the first time, I felt like my life was moving forwards, not backwards.

Realising My Purpose

Working with people who had been through trauma, addiction, prison, homelessness — I saw myself in all of them. I knew their struggles, their fears, their silent battles. My past wasn't a burden anymore. It was a bridge.

Every day, I helped people find their footing, rebuild their

 36

confidence, and believe in their worth. And the more I helped others,

37

the more I discovered my own strength.

For the first time, I wasn't surviving. I was living. I was growing. I was showing up — for them, and for me.

They didn't just offer me a job; they offered me belief. That belief changed everything.

A New Chapter

My time at "Eco-Actif" came to an end,

Meeting someone special in Eastbourne changed the direction of my life again. Moving to East Sussex felt like closing an old chapter and opening a new one — one with more peace, more possibility, more truth.

Leaving Surrey wasn't running away. It was choosing something better for myself.

In Eastbourne, I began looking into services for people coming out of prison — and I was shocked by what I found. Or, rather, by what wasn't there.

Almost nothing. No real support. No structure. No hope.

I knew what that felt like — to walk out of prison with nothing but a travel card, a bag, and fear. I knew how close that emptiness could push someone back into the same cycle.

I couldn't ignore it. So I didn't

That hit me hard. I knew how much of a difference it had made for me to have someone believe in me. I couldn't just sit back and do nothing. So I decided to change that.

That's when Reformed East Sussex was born — out of a laptop, a desk, and a dream bigger than me.

But even as Reformed grew, even as I helped others rebuild their lives and spoke about hope and change…

Something inside me was still unfinished. I had helped people find who they were. But I had not yet fully claimed who I was.

That truth was waiting for me. Quietly. Patiently.

And when it finally came forward, I knew:

This — living my truth — was the biggest transformation of

 38

all. I was so proud of what we achieved.

39

We opened a second office in Hastings and created new opportunities for so many who had been written off by society. We gave people a safe space to rebuild — to rediscover their worth.

Reformed wasn't just a service; it was a family, a movement, a message that change is possible.

But even as the work grew, something inside me was still missing.

I was helping others find themselves — yet, deep down, I still hadn't fully found me.

"You don't just go through life — you grow through it." — Unknown

40

41

Chapter 6

Closing Reflections

Reformed East Sussex had grown into something bigger than I ever imagined. What started as one person, one laptop, and one small windowless office had become a lifeline for so many people — people who felt lost, unheard, judged, or forgotten. I poured everything I had into it: my heart, my past, my strength, and the belief that no one is ever too broken to rebuild.

But even while I was helping others find themselves, a quiet truth inside me kept pulling me closer. It was something I had carried for years — hidden, suppressed, pushed down by fear and circumstances. I had rebuilt my life, but I hadn't yet rebuilt myself.

For so long, I'd avoided mirrors because the person staring back felt like a stranger. My reflection never matched the person I felt like on the inside. I had lived decades trying to survive a life that didn't fit me, trying to be who the world expected, not who I truly was.

I could help others walk toward their truth, but I still hadn't stepped fully into mine.

After a few years of living in Eastbourne, settling into the quiet routines of coastal life, I met a beautiful woman — someone who felt unlike anyone I had ever known. She wasn't chaotic, unpredictable, or carrying storms inside her like so many people from my past. She was calm. Grounded. Steady in a way that made me feel both seen and safe. For the first time in my life, I experienced what "normal" could look like — and it was disarming in the most unexpected way.

She showed me what real love was without ever needing to say the words outright. It was in her gentleness, in the way she listened, in the way she touched my hand as if she understood the parts of me I didn't yet have language for. I wasn't used to someone who didn't

42

want to fix me, judge me, or question every part of who I was. Instead, she met me with patience — a patience I didn't believe I deserved at the time. Slowly, over weeks, months, and eventually years, we fell in love. A love built on quiet moments, shared routines, and a steadiness I had never experienced before.

But even within that peace, a part of me was unravelling on the inside. After seven years together, a restlessness began to grow — something I couldn't ignore anymore. I wasn't unhappy with her; she had been nothing but good to me. I was unhappy with myself. There was something unresolved inside me, something I had buried so deeply over a lifetime of survival, shame, and pretending, that I had convinced myself it was gone. But it wasn't. It was waiting for its moment to speak, and eventually it began to shout louder than everything else.

I felt guilty for feeling that way. Guilty for not being able to explain what was wrong. Guilty for holding a secret I couldn't fully understand myself. I remember lying awake at night feeling like I was living in a body that wasn't mine, a life that didn't quite fit, a version of myself I had outgrown long before I even met her. It was confusing, painful, and terrifying.

With a heavy heart — one filled with sadness, fear, and the weight of a truth I could no longer hide from — I made the decision to leave. It was the hardest thing I had ever done, because I wasn't walking away from her. I was walking toward myself. Toward a truth that had been whispering inside me for decades, waiting for the moment I was strong enough to listen.

Leaving wasn't about losing her. It was about finally choosing me.

It was during that time, in the quiet space that followed the breakup, that everything inside me became clear. The fog lifted. The truth stood bare. I finally understood why nothing in my life had ever felt aligned, why my reflection felt wrong, why no amount of love or stability could quiet the ache inside me.

And so I began my transition — from female to male — not as an act of becoming someone new, but as an act of returning to the

 43

person I had always been. It was the beginning of my real life. The first time I allowed myself to breathe without pretending. The first time I had the courage to step into my own truth.

Transitioning didn't erase the past or the love I had shared. It honoured it. Because choosing to be myself meant choosing to live honestly, fully, and without shame.

It was the moment I stopped surviving and finally started living

Taking the First Steps

The first steps were terrifying. Not because I didn't know who I was, but because I did — and I feared the world's reaction to that truth.

Transitioning wasn't just a decision. It was an act of returning to myself.

It meant peeling back years of silence, years of trying to survive in a life that didn't reflect who I truly was. It meant confronting the judgements, the whispers, the assumptions. It meant risking rejection. It meant risking everything I'd built.

But it also meant freedom. Real freedom. A freedom I had never experienced — not in childhood, not on the streets, not in prisons, not in hostels.

A freedom that wasn't about where I lived, but who I was allowed to be.

 44

Change had always been my message — yet this was the biggest change of all.

The one that meant living honestly, completely, as the person I had always been meant to be.

It wasn't an easy journey. There were days of fear, uncertainty, and judgement, but there were also days of freedom and quiet joy — moments when I could finally breathe without hiding.

Transitioning wasn't about becoming someone new; it was about returning to myself.

It was about truth, and truth is never wrong.

As I began to live openly, I found that my message carried even more power. People would say,

"You're proof that you can rebuild from anything."

And maybe I am.

I've stood in the darkest corners of life and somehow found the light. I've seen the worst in people — and the best. I've lost everything and built it again, stronger each time.

Now, I live in that light.

I use my voice to help others see that they can too.

I take photographs — capturing small, fleeting moments of truth.

Because a picture can say what words sometimes can't. It holds a thousand emotions in one breath, and that's what my life has become

— a series of moments that prove change, beauty, and hope can coexist.

The Journey Home to Myself

Transitioning wasn't an overnight moment. It was a slow unfolding

45

— like finally allowing myself to breathe after holding my breath for years. It wasn't about becoming someone new. It was about returning to the person I had always been inside. It was about truth, and truth is never wrong.

46

There were days of fear, days where I questioned whether I was strong enough to face the world as myself. There were moments where cuts from the past reopened, moments where judgement stung more sharply than any physical pain I'd survived.

But there were also days of peace — gentle, quiet moments where I looked in the mirror and finally recognised the person looking back.

Moments where I smiled without forcing it. Moments where I felt alignment, lightness, and relief I had never experienced before.

There were days I felt like a child learning how to walk again — learning how to speak, dress, and exist as myself. But each step brought me closer to a life that finally felt like mine.

Becoming a Voice

As I lived more openly and truthfully, something unexpected happened. My story began to touch people even more deeply. I wasn't just speaking about change — I was living it. The people I supported saw that transformation wasn't just a word; it was proof.

I remember someone saying to me:

"You show us that no matter where you start, you can still become who you were meant to be."

Maybe that's what my life has been all along — a series of returns.

Returning to hope. Returning to strength. And finally, returning to myself.

I've stood in some of the darkest corners of life — addiction, violence, homelessness, prison, loss. I've seen the worst parts of humanity… but also the best. I've seen people rise from places they never thought they'd escape. I've seen light grow in the most unexpected places.

And now I live in that light.

Photography — Capturing Truth

As my life evolved, so did the way I expressed myself. I started taking photographs — not just pictures, but moments. Small, fleeting pockets of truth that spoke louder than words.

Photography became another form of healing. A way to freeze

 47

beauty, hope, strength, identity — all the things I had once believed I'd never have. Each photograph was a reminder that life could be soft, honest, full of meaning.

48

A camera doesn't judge. It doesn't question. It captures what is — and sometimes, that is enough.

My pictures became reflections of the world I had fought so hard to reach. Moments that proved that change, resilience, and hope could coexist.

The Courage to Be Myself

Transitioning didn't fix everything, but it aligned everything. I no longer felt like I was carrying a secret inside me. I no longer felt like I was pretending to be someone I wasn't. Every day, I grew more into the person I had kept hidden throughout my childhood, my teenage years, and the chaos that followed.

And with every step I took toward myself, the world around me began to shift too.

People would tell me:

"You're proof that no matter how dark the past, there's always a way forward."

And maybe they're right. Maybe that's who I am — not just a survivor, but a reminder that rebuilding is possible.

A Life Rebuilt from the Ground Up

I've lost everything before. I've rebuilt everything from scratch. And I've learned that strength isn't about how much pain you can endure. It's about how many times you choose to rise.

My past no longer defines me. It informs me, strengthens me, guides me — but it no longer controls me.

I live openly now. I speak my truth. I help others become who they're meant to be. And I do it because I know what it feels like to be lost, unheard, unseen.

I know what it feels like to look for yourself in a world that doesn't understand you.

My Truth, My Message

Today, my mission is simple: to show others what I once needed someone to show me — that there is always hope, even when you can't see it. That change is possible, even when you don't believe it. That transformation isn't just for other people — it's for you too.

49

Because if I can see it, I can do it. And if I can do it — rising from trauma, from prison, from the streets, from self-doubt, from living in a

50

body that never felt like home — then so can you.

"The courage to be yourself is the beginning of all transformation."
— Roman Sewell

If I can see it, I can do it. And
if I can do it, so can you.
"The courage to be yourself is the beginning of all transformation."
— Roman Sewell

51

A Surreal Moment

Visiting Parliament was something I never imagined in my wildest dreams.

I remember walking down the long corridor towards the Home Secretary's office, my heart pounding in disbelief.

The huge doors opened, and there I was — sitting around her enormous table, in a place where decisions were made about people like me.

I thought back to Holloway Prison, to the girl who had lost all

hope. Now I was here, being listened to, respected, valued.

52

It was surreal.

53

And in that moment, I felt something I hadn't felt in years — proud.

Eventually, my time with Reformed East Sussex came to an end.

The service closed, but not because of failure — rather, it had fulfilled its purpose.

To rebuild what was broken, to remind people that change is possible.

And as one chapter ended, another began — my journey of hope, healing, and giving back.

About the Author

Roman Sewell is a writer, advocate, and founder of several community-driven projects designed to support people who have experienced trauma, marginalization, or exclusion. His work is rooted in lived experience — a powerful journey of survival, resilience, growth, and transformation that has shaped him into the person he is today.

Born into hardship and raised in chaos, Roman's early life was marked by instability, violence, and years spent navigating homelessness, addiction, exploitation, and the criminal justice

54

system.

55

Yet even in the darkest moments, he held onto a small spark of hope
— a spark that would eventually ignite a remarkable path of rebuilding, healing, and purpose.

After overcoming the challenges of prison, poverty, and identity struggles, Roman dedicated his life to supporting those who walk the same difficult roads he once did. His work began with volunteering and grew into a career helping people in recovery, ex-offenders, and individuals facing barriers to education, employment, and stability. Roman became known not only for his compassion, but for his ability to meet people where they are — with honesty, understanding, and lived wisdom.

Roman later founded Reformed East Sussex, a community organisation built from nothing but determination, a small desk, and a dream to give people leaving prison the support he never had. Under his leadership, Reformed became a recognised and respected service across the county, reaching countless people who felt forgotten or judged by society.

As Roman continued rebuilding his life, he stepped into his truth as a transgender man — a journey that deepened his purpose and strengthened his voice. His own transition became a message of authenticity and courage, inspiring others to live honestly and unapologetically. Roman believes that identity is not a limitation but a liberation, and that every person deserves the chance to live as who they truly are.

He is also the creator of the Transgender Rock Project, a community initiative providing peer support, mentoring, and pathways into education, training, and employment for transgender people across the UK. Through this project, Roman works to create safe spaces for people to grow, learn, and reconnect with their own strengths.

Beyond his community work, Roman is a passionate photographer, capturing raw and powerful images that reflect truth, emotion, and the beauty found within everyday moments. His photography and writing both serve as creative expressions of healing — ways of telling stories that words alone can't always

56

hold.

Roman now shares his story through public speaking, advocacy, mentoring, and his writing. His voice carries a simple but

57

life-changing message:

No matter where you begin, you can rebuild. No matter how lost you feel, there is always a way forward. If you can see it, you can do it.

Roman continues to inspire others by showing that transformation is not only possible — it is powerful

■ Contact: roman.sewell1@gmail.com

 58

Printed in Dunstable, United Kingdom

74885334R00063